Dr. Christopher Blythe on Mormon Apocalypticism

Introduction

Dr. Christopher Blythe is a Research Associate at the Maxwell Institute at BYU and author of "Terrible Revolution." We will learn more about his role at the Maxwell Institute and learn more about end-times beliefs of Latter-day Saints over the past 2 centuries from Joseph Smith, right up to modern times with people like Julie Rowe and Chad Daybell. Check out our conversation....

Tags: Gospel Tangents, Rick Bennett, LDS Church, Latter-day Saints, LDS Church, Mormon, Mormon Church, Church of Jesus Christ of Latter-day Saints, Mormon history, Mormon, LDS Church, LDS, Church of Latter Day Saints, Christopher Blythe, Terrible Revolution, apocalypse, apocalypticism, millennium, millenarianism, end times, Chad Daybell, Julie Rowe, Bo Gritz, Joseph Smith, Utah War, White Horse Prophecy, scholars, Brigham Young, Maxwell Institute, Joseph Smith, Mitt Romney, Lori Vallow, murder, Pontius, Visions of Glory, Civil War Prophecy, Maxwell Institute, FARMS, the Interpreter,

Contents

Maxwell Institute: A Religious Thinktank

Introduction

I'm excited to introduce Dr. Christopher Blythe or the Maxwell Institute. We'll get acquainted with him, learn more about the Maxwell Institute, and even find out more about their collaborative relationship with the Interpreter group. Check out our conversation....

Interview

GT 00:04 Welcome to *Gospel Tangents*. I'm excited to be here at the Neal A. Maxwell Institute. We're at the brand-new building, and I have an awesome guest. Could you go ahead and tell us who you are?

Christopher 00:14 I'm Christopher James Blythe.

GT 00:16 And you have a great new book.

Christopher 00:17 Yeah, I am the author of *Terrible Revolution: Latter-day Saints and the American Apocalypse* that just came out. I'm also a research associate at the Maxwell Institute here.

GT 00:27 That's great. So that's a big question I have. I also want to get your academic background. I think you went to school with Don Bradley up at Utah State. Is that right?

Christopher 00:36 Yes, that's right.

GT 00:38 Where did you get your bachelor's? Where did you get your masters and all that, and Ph.D.?

Christopher 00:43 I started at Texas A&M University.

GT 00:45 Oh, you're an Aggie.

Christopher 00:46 Yeah, I'm twice an Aggie.[1]

GT 00:49 Yeah, that's right.

Christopher 00:50 That's right. So in 1999, I started school there. I finished in 2003, with a degree in anthropology. Then, it was my last year at Texas A&M that I discovered my love of religious studies. So I took that last year, really, just taking religion classes, and 2004 hit. Although I'd kind of wondered whether I was going to go on a mission or not, I went on a mission in 2004, and I came back in 2006. When I came back, I just worked at a bookstore. Then I heard that Phil Barlow was taking a spot at Utah State. I knew my grades from Texas A&M weren't going to get me into grad school. So I got a second bachelor's degree at Utah State with Phil Barlow in Religious Studies, and moved right into the master's program there in history. My second year there, that's when Don Bradley came. [There was a] great little group of Mormon Studies students and scholars that have come out of that program. Before us, guys like Mark Ashurst-McGee and my former boss at the Joseph Smith Papers,[2] Matt Godfrey went to USU, too. There's quite a number of different scholars have come out of that Utah State master's program. So pretty neat. Then from there, I went to Florida State did my PhD work there in American Religious History.

GT 02:31 The Seminoles.

Christopher 02:34 That's right.

GT 02:35 So are you a big football fan?

---

[1] Both Utah State and Texas A&M are known as Aggies.
[2] See https://www.josephsmithpapers.org/

Christopher 02:37 I am not. In fact, I had to stop and say, "Wait a second. Is that right? Are they the Seminoles?"

Christopher 02:43 So no, not at all.

GT 02:45 Wow. Interesting. So yeah, my first companion was from College Station, Texas. He wasn't my first. I was his first companion. I trained him. So I learned more than I wanted to know about Texas A&M football.

Christopher 02:59 It's a big deal. It's a really big deal there. So Texas A&M and Florida State, football is everything. I went to one Texas A&M game, and I don't think I ever went to a Florida State game.

GT 03:10 Wow. I've actually been to a Florida State game.

Christopher 03:13 Is that right? Nice.

GT 03:15 Yeah, it's pretty cool. I haven't been to A&M, I did go to a TCU one.

Christopher 03:20 Nice.

GT 03:21 Well, cool, well, we won't talk anymore football. You were a convert. Is that right?

Christopher 03:26 Yes.

GT 03:27 Were you a member at Texas A&M? Did you grow up in Texas, or where did you grow up?

Christopher 03:32 My father was in the Army and so he went to Texas A&M, and my brother went to Texas A&M. So there was a definite link there in Texas, but we grew up all around--Hawaii and Korea...

GT 03:44 Oh, Hawaii, that would be nice.

Christopher 03:48 So I joined the church in Burke, Virginia, when I was 13. I finished seminary. I then moved away and went to college. While I was at college, I joined a fraternity. So instead of getting ready to go on my mission, I got ready to get really involved in social life at Texas A&M, and so I was still a member, but I didn't go to church while I was in college, except for sporadically, except for that last year. Then I thought, "All right, I've got to get things in order."

GT 04:24 Well, cool. So I also have a question about the Neal A. Maxwell Institute. You're a research - what's your official title?

Christopher 04:33 I'm a Research Associate. I'm actually...

GT 04:35 Research Associate. Do you do any teaching at BYU here, or not really?

Christopher 04:38 No, just if I want to. I taught a class in 2019 for the Religion Department. What did they call it? [It was] sort of, Church History/Doctrine and Covenants merged together. I forget the name. [It was] Gospel Foundations. So I like teaching, but I also love having this time to write. So this is a great spot to research and write and they hook you up with great student researchers to help you with your projects and fund you to go visit different sites and different archives.

GT 05:14 Sounds like a dream job!

Christopher 05:15 It is a dream job. There's no question. The position I'm in right now they are hiring another scholar for next year. I have one more year, but another scholar is going to join us next year. So applications are due in a month. So if I was not me, I would be applying furiously, if I had a project, particularly on the

Book of Mormon. The spot I'm in is for the Willis Center, so it's funding specifically for Book of Mormon research.

GT 05:46 So can we think of this as kind of a think tank? Like, we have political think tanks? Is this a religious think tank?

Christopher 05:52 Yes. I think that's probably right. We all have our own different projects. Then we meet together, brainstorm together on--read each other's writings. Sometimes, there's a project that comes from above that those that actually work here might be part of or might not be. So, right now, brief theological introductions to the Book of Mormon have been the big thing. One of us wrote a volume for it. These are these wonderful little 30,000-word books, each on a different book in the Book of Mormon. Those of us that are here, I think only Deidre wrote a volume for it. Deidre is one of the other scholars actually just finished her time here. So, it's actually a think tank, not just for those of us that are full time here, but sometimes others are pulled in to be part of that.

GT 06:56 Do you sign on here for a set number of years?

Christopher 06:59 There's all sorts of different positions here. So, we have more permanent individuals, of course, like Philip Barlow or...

GT 07:07 I was going to say. Did he follow you? Or did you follow him?

Christopher 07:10 I followed him. I followed Dr. Barlow everywhere. My first spot out of Florida State was his sabbatical replacement. I spent a year filling his shoes at Utah State. So I have followed him all around. I spent three years at *Joseph Smith Papers*, and then an opening happened here. So I came right over. So yes, I've definitely been following him.

Christopher 07:34 [There are] all sorts of different positions here. Some of them are permanent. So Terryl Givens is permanent here, and Christian Heel, a scholar of Syriac Christianity. But for the most part, we're in the sort of three-year spots, and that would be Janiece Johnson and myself. They're all staggered on when people began, as well as a wonderful scholar, Catherine Taylor, who works on art history of early Christianity. Fiona Givens is here on a three year spot. Of course, we also have Spencer Fluhman, who's here from the history department, leading us for a four-year term, and hopefully another four-year term. It's all a great institute here. It's going to keep in flux, a lot of scholars are going to come through and get this opportunity to have time to write. It's exciting. Usually people have one sabbatical year, maybe they've been in their tenure track position for seven years. But it's not until they're really into their career they have time to write. So the idea that BYU has a spot for religious studies, religious scholarship, where somebody in their 30s, or 40s, could come, or younger, even and have three years to actually get books written is incredible. It's unheard of.

GT 08:58 Well, yes, and you've got a great book, *Terrible Revolution*. It's fantastic.

Christopher 09:04 Thank you.

GT 09:05 So, yes, I just finished that and I'm excited to talk about that. Before we do, though. I just wanted to ask one other question. I know, Daniel Peterson in the FARMS group used to be part of the Neal A. Maxwell [Institute.] Can you talk a little bit about that transition?

Christopher 09:18 It's before my time. I think there were concerns. The thing is, I only know about it at the same level that everyone else before our time knows about it. I think there were questions about how we should be pursuing the scholarship. When I heard Daniel Peterson was removed and [I] read all those things, I was concerned. I thought, "Wait a second. Shouldn't there be spots for all sorts of voices in this conversation?" That's still how I feel, and so I'm really happy that there's a better relationship. I published an article in *The Interpreter*[3] just a couple months ago.

GT 09:59 Yes, because FARMS, I guess I should probably [explain that.] Some people won't know what FARMS even stands for: Foundation of Ancient Research and Mormon Studies. That was started 20-30 years ago probably.[4] I think BYU kind of absorbed FARMS, and then it became the Neal Maxwell Institute. Then Dan Peterson, and some of those original FARMS people started *The Interpreter*.

Christopher 10:23 Yes, so there are kind of a couple of heirs of that early FARMS. I think we're one of those heirs, The *Neal A Maxwell Institute*. Another heir is *Book of Mormon Central*, that Jack Welch has headed up. Another heir is *The Interpreter* of that early legacy. I think what we do now is more, sort of, we're studying the richness and the theology of the Book of Mormon. We're looking at reception history. We're writing both towards the Church and for the academy. We're not doing—when there are moments that we can move in and handle a major issue that people are debating, we participate in conversations about the importance of the Book of Mormon, why Latter-day Saints should read it, larger subjects like that. But it's unlikely that we would write a response to the CES Letter or something out of here now, today. I think there's a place for that. It's even something I might be interested in doing at some point. So I'm glad that there are spots such as *The Interpreter* and *Book of Mormon Central*, where that could occur, even though it's not occurring here in a university environment, and I think that makes sense too.

---

[3] See https://interpreterfoundation.org/

[4] FARMS was founded in 1979 by John Welch in California. It was a private, not-for-profit organization. In 1997, FARMS was invited to become part of BYU by President Hinckley. In 2006 it was renamed the Neal A. Maxwell Institute for Religious Scholarship. In 2012, BYU removed Daniel Peterson as editor of the *Mormon Studies Review* an in an acrimonious split. Peterson resigned from the Maxwell Institute and went on to found a new private group called *The Interpreter*.

GT 11:49 So would you say that *Interpreter* is more of an apologetic bent, and you guys are more of a Religious Studies bent? Is that fair?

Christopher 11:54 I think there's a--what we want to do here is faithful Religious Studies scholarship. So, absolutely, we're believers. We're very much on the side of the Church. However, we're scholars. So we're going to dig in, and we talk to our field as well. So, what's really important to us is to speak those two languages, both of the academy and to the Saints, rather than just focus on one of those areas. Lots of times, people will bring up a philosophy that, today, as we're defending the church, we don't want to do so defensively. So we're not doing it on the terms of the Church's critics. We're not answering each of these pinpoints. We're not focused necessarily on "why did Nephi's bow break," or some question like that, right? Instead, we're looking at how can early Latter-day Saint theology apply to modern day problems, or how does the Book of Mormon address issues like racism, or sexism, and so on? So that takes a different approach. An interesting thing is when I started working here, we still had this wonderful FARMS stone. Did you ever see this?

GT 13:18 No.

Christopher 13:19 This is, I don't know how you would describe it. It's really this carved statue of the FARMS logo, that must have weighed a ton, in front of our building.

GT 13:29 Yes, you're in a new building, now.

Christopher 13:30 We are in a new building, and it's wonderful. We gave that to Book of Mormon Central, so they came out and got some heavy equipment to move this thing over to their property in Springville. So we have a great relationship with all of these guys. I hope so. I know that there can be bad blood from a different generation of scholars. But I think our younger generation actually is getting along much better and really, all of the institutions that FARMS has.

GT 14:04 There's no real rivalry between *Interpreter* and the *Maxwell Institute* anymore.

Christopher 14:07 Well, I've never thought of that. Yes, I don't see that. I would think the issues that happened before were actually pre-Spencer Fluhman. These are things that almost all the scholars here, it predates, which is important to remember. I think one of the unfortunate things is because some of that controversy was so public, it means that people don't actually know the players involved, and they just say *Maxwell* and *Interpreter*. Whereas, I don't think anyone here had any voice in any of those conversations.

GT 14:45 Well, it's interesting that you said you've written some stuff for *The Interpreter*, too, so that shows some collaboration.

Christopher 14:51 Yes.

GT 14:52 I know this isn't really your expertise, but I still want to ask it. Utah State has a Mormon Studies program. University of Utah has Mormon Studies. USC, I think is just starting one. Claremont has one, University of Virginia. Why does BYU not have a Mormon Studies program? Wouldn't they be the Notre Dame of Mormon Studies?

Christopher 15:13 Yes. Oh, I'm so grateful. If you wanted to come to BYU and study Mormon Studies, you could certainly get a Comparative Studies Master's program and work with great scholars. You could get a degree in the English department. We have a great scholar here, who does Latter-day Saint folklore, Eric Eliason. I think he's probably who I would work under, if I was not going to Utah State, or who I'd try to work under. So I think there's some outlets there. The history department at BYU once had a Ph.D. Then they got rid of their Ph.D. They went to a master's and now they only have an undergraduate program. BYU really wants to focus on the undergraduate.

GT 15:58 I know Alex Baugh, I talked to him.[5] He got a Ph.D. from BYU in history.

Christopher 16:01 Right. So there was this brief moment. There's a great crop of guys who came there. Kent Godfrey a great Latter-day Saints scholar got his Ph.D. here. There's a handful of others. But they ended these programs. So, really, I don't know where we would put that. We'd call it Latter-day Saints Studies, but where would we put that Latter-day Saints studies chair, right? So, the great thing is we have--I mean, obviously this would be the place to get your undergraduate if you wanted to focus on LDS history. I mean, because you have this--the religion department is full of really impressive scholars. They've got guys like J.B. Haws and Scott Esplin has a great book.

GT 16:43 I'll have to get J.B. on my podcast. He's a great scholar.

Christopher 16:46 He is a great scholar. I'm a big fan of Mike McKay and Gerrit Dirkmaat, Nick Fredrickson and Joseph Spencer. I mean, there's really just this great core there. Whereas, if I was an undergraduate thinking, "I want to go to grad school," in Latter-day Saint studies, I would think BYU is the place to go. I think that's what BYU wants to be known as, somebody who sort of prepares undergraduates to go off and pursue their graduate degrees elsewhere. Now, if that ever changed, it would also be a great thing.

GT 17:16 Well, I'm just going to put in my opinion. I think BYU should have a Latter-day Saint Studies program.

Christopher 17:22 I like it.

---

[5] See our interview at https://gospeltangents.com/category/alex-baugh/

GT 17:24 <u>I mentioned it to Elder Snow</u>,[6] even, and he said he would put a word in, but I don't know that it'll go anywhere.

Christopher 17:28 Yes, I like it. This is a great spot. You can't take classes with Philip Barlow, and you can't take classes with [Terryl.] Actually, Terryl Givens taught a class last year. Spencer teaches a class every couple years, Terryl taught a class last year in English and Spencer in history. I don't think Dr. Barlow has, but it's still a great--there's an awesome opportunity we have both for our master's students and our undergrads is the *Maxwell Institute* is always hiring student researchers. It's a pretty amazing deal. So they're paid pretty well. They're paid much more than I was paid as a researcher as an undergrad. They're given 20 hours a week, sort of thing, and it's a great experience. So each of us have, two or three undergraduate or Master's student researchers who get hands on training. We do our best to mentor. I'm sure some of us are better mentors than others. It's pretty great. The latest Ph.D. student at University of Virginia, a guy named Stephen Betts who's also just started a podcast, *Scholars and Saints* at UVA or *Saints with Scholars*, I'm not sure which. He was Philip Barlow's research assistant for a couple years and so, although he didn't do his master's degree in Mormon Studies, he did it in linguistics. But he had this hands-on relationship with a mentor that really was Mormon Studies right before he went off to study at the big times with Kathleen Flake at the University of Virginia.

---

[6] See https://gospeltangents.com/2019/08/does-church-hide-documents/

Mormon History of Apocalypse

Introduction

Apocalyptism has been important to Latter-day Saint theology and is why we're called Latter-day Saints. In our next conversation with Dr. Christopher Blythe, we'll get an overview of his book, *Terrible Revolution*, and learn more about LDS Apocalyptic thought over the past two centuries. Check out our conversation....

Interview

GT 19:05 Okay. Cool. All right. Well, let's dive into your book. Why don't you go ahead and show everybody this wonderful book, *Terrible Revolution*. I have to tell you, when I think of the apocalypse, I always think of [The Book of] Revelation and everybody's going to die. So, that's kind of what I expected your book to be. It was really interesting to see that it was--like the apocalypse you always think of as in the future, but you actually looked at it as a lens from the past and went through a lot of different time periods. So how did you get interested in Mormon apocalypticism. I can't even say that word. Actually, you'd mentioned it's different than Millenarianism. I can't even say that word either. So can you talk a little bit about that?

Christopher 19:57 Yes. There's a great book by Grant Underwood, The Millenarian World of Early Mormonism.[7] [It's a] brilliant book, and one of the things it did was talk about Latter-day Saint last days thoughts in context of Christian theology. Grant will walk us through and say, "Post-millennialism is different than millenarianism, or what we call pre-millennialism." When you're a post millennialist, you think things are going great. Society is going to get better and better and better, and then the Savior will appear, perhaps, and you'll be in the millennium. It'll be a wonderful--and

---

[7] Can be purchased at https://amzn.to/3n1AEki

sometimes it's seen more symbolically, so the Savior doesn't necessarily appear in the same way. But, it's human invention, a human turning towards Christ. It just perfects the world. Pre-millennialists or millenarians have a perspective that--it's what we're more used to seeing. The world is going to get worse and worse and worse, then Jesus shows up. Destructions happen. The righteous are selected, and then the Millennium happens. So, Grant Underwood makes a point to say that Latter-day Saints, even though we have utopian ideas, like building Zion as an essential part before the Savior comes, really, we're millenarians. We expect society to crumble before the Millennium happens. So, it's not by human invention. There's a great talk from Joseph Smith. Some people argue nowadays, when we're trying to pick apart what Joseph wrote and what W.W. Phelps wrote, so some people say Phelps wrote this, but it's a great editorial called *The Kingdom of God*. It's published in 1842. It starts out with Joseph saying, "The world has had 6000 years to try to run a free government for the good. In the last thousand years, God, Himself, is going to set this straight and lead us."

Christopher 21:57 It's a beautiful message, I think. So, Joseph's trying to bring that out in his career as he starts the Council of Fifty and others. "What's the government of God look like?" That's sort of the message of millenarianism. Right? Human beings are limited in their capacity. God certainly has an elect people, but it's going to take God's intervention in humanity to set us straight.

Christopher: So when I talk about apocalypticism, I'm trying to skirt that whole conversation. I think Mormon Studies scholars, for a couple decades, were spending so much of their time having conversations about, "How does Mormonism relate to Christianity?" Even somebody like Jan Shipps, or Philip Barlow, or Terryl Givens, or Grant Underwood are trying to position Mormonism into this evangelical frame. I'm less interested in that. So I wanted to jump in and say, "Yes, we're millenarians. Don't worry about it. But what I want to talk about is apocalypticism." That is the sort of on-the-ground disasters that Latter-day Saints are expecting and participating in. I use a term that a great scholar, Catherine Wessinger, uses to describe this. Instead of millenarianism, I talk about catastrophic apocalypticism. So we are waiting around. [No,] we're not waiting around. We're participant in all these wonderful, building Zion ideas, doing missionary work, work for the dead, that we believe prepares the world for the Second Coming. But, also, there's a sort of emphasis, which is what I looked at, of destructions. The world is going to erupt. These corrupt governments, which from an early Latter-day Saint view is all governments, will collapse. So, we're waiting for that to occur.

GT 22:13 All right. So walk us through the book a little bit. How do you start out? Because you take this, from Joseph Smith's day, right up to the present, pretty much. We are Latter-day Saints, and there's a reason why we call ourselves Latter-day Saints.

Christopher 24:03 That's right. I think, when I write about apocalypticism, I look at it as a lens that has been present among Latter-day Saints even before the Church is officially formed. So, one of the things I try to do here is move in right with Joseph Smith's encounters with Moroni and see how a lens of the Book of Revelation, biblical prophecy really plays into our story, the story of our faith. Joseph isn't going to talk about the First Vision as this founding moment until later. This is held back, often, when he teaches it. He's always starting with a story about Moroni, the coming of these plates. I think that story has always been steeped in, even the idea of this special book, a sealed record is alluded-- there are sealed records in the Book of Revelation. The idea of an angel coming with the gospel of the last days, Joseph sees in the Book of Revelation and so on. I think it has that apocalyptic lens right from the beginning.

Christopher 25:08 So what I do is, I'm a folklorist. I'm a cultural historian, too. But what I want to do is not stop and say, "This is the official story of The Church of Jesus Christ of Latter-day Saints." If you're a missionary, you go out and you want to clarify to everybody, "No, Latter-day Saints believe this". Somebody says,

"Wait, you believe it kind of this way?" You say, "No, no, no, it's really this way." You have very, very set views that you want people to understand [that] Latter-day Saints have. That's not how it works on the ground. Latter-day Saints have a variety of views that change based on the time period you're living with, based on where people are living, based on individual preferences and individual emphasis, individual experience.

Christopher 25:57 So the first chapter is about the master narrative. This is the story that Joseph Smith tells. It's about the basic themes of apocalyptic that Latter-day Saints are going to play with. These are ideas such as the importance of the gathering, the importance of the restoration of Lamanites, the idea of the gospel going to the world, the idea of a millennium that's going to happen, a return to Jackson County, the idea that persecution and martyrdom is a key to this. [These ideas include] all sorts of basic things; the role that the temple has to play and last days' expectations. Once I try to establish that scene there, I then try to talk about how in each new setting, the Saints are returning to this sort of master narrative, and it's dynamic. So, it's changing and evolving. Church leaders, sometimes--this is a main point, is to either sort of let the members loose in doing whatever they want with this message: sharing visions and speculating themselves in the apocalypse, which I argue is useful sometimes.

Christopher 27:09 And other times pulling them back saying, "Hey, let's not talk about future Messianic prophecies or prophets coming forth to lead us back to Jackson County. Let's leave that alone. Or let's leave alone the idea that Native Americans will have uprisings. Those things are more dangerous. Let's not talk about them right now." And then that moves through time. So, the first chapter is on that master narrative. The second chapter moves into the importance of martyrdom from Joseph Smith. What does Joseph Smith's death look like for the Saints? The third chapter is on how geography plays into the story of the Mormon apocalyptic, not only what Jackson County or the Americas played in that story, but also once they arrive in the Rocky Mountains. What does that look like? Of course, I expect many listeners will realize, the Rocky Mountains under Brigham Young was a fulfillment of prophecies of Isaiah, and things like Ensign Peak or a 'last days' temple built here. But I show how that apocalyptic geography goes down to Mexico or up to Canada, depending on where the Saints are. If you serve a mission in England, Parley P. Pratt, is going to go to Queen Victoria and say, "Hey, you're no exception. Prophecy says all thrones are going to be cast down, and so you need to know England also is part of the story." I then move on to chapter four, called The Judgments Begin: Apocalypticism in the Utah Territory. This is about how the Utah War and federal prosecution of polygamists and the Civil War itself, all festered ideas of apocalypticism.

Christopher 29:04 Particularly at this point, Latter-day Saints' leaders really encouraged people to participate in apocalypticism. So, over the pulpit, we heard folk prophecies, lay prophecies from individual members predicting the destruction of the soldiers attacking, or individuals sharing their dreams in newspapers of how near the Second Coming was happening. [It was] always addressed towards the nation, particularly, as we become more concerned that the nation is these last-days tyrants, attacking Utah, the faithful. It plays out in these visions and stories.

Christopher 29:44 One of the things [that] I think is so interesting in this period, is that the battle of Armageddon, this major event, and apocalypticism that we see in Ezekiel and the Book of Revelation. It's set in the Bible, very specifically in Palestine in the fields of Armageddon. Latter-day Saints still think that's the case. But the story of armies surrounding Israel is really the story. Then God fights the Battle of Israel. The armies all get taken out. That sort of foreign invasion, by the evil Pirate King is now portrayed as occurring in Utah. People are expecting how God is going to defend them from this last wave of attackers. Then everything changes. In 1896, statehood is granted to Utah. So, this fifth chapter is Americanization: a Mormon Apocalyptic, where Latter-day Saint leaders begin to discourage the things that were so popular before.

Christopher 30:52 I think it's fascinating. George Q. Cannon, we're really lucky that we now have access to George Q. Cannon's diaries through the Church.[8] Just recently, probably one of the first books that uses them. In 1896, when statehood is announced, George Q. Cannon writes, "I now know how these prophecies are going to be fulfilled. If we were going to protect the Constitution, we can't do it on our own out there. We have to be part of this nation." So, now things get rethought of. On one hand, Church leaders crack down on folk prophecy. On the other, they begin to reimagine--what's prophecy look like if we're not predicting these bad things happen to America, but we actually are part of America?

Christopher 31:37 Then finally, in Chapter Six, it's called 20th and 21st Century Apocalyptic Traditions, or Trajectories. This traces three different streams of how millennial thought continues to the present. So, Grant Underwood would talk about moderate millenarianism, to describe Latter-day Saints, to say they're not really radical, and they had this sort of consistent ideas of last-days belief that emphasized sort of the millennium, and various other elements and that haven't changed much. So, I say one of these trajectories could be called modern millenarianism. That's sort of the trajectory of the institution of The Church of Jesus Christ of Latter-day Saints. In that version, you're no longer picking out your enemies. You're not predicting judgments on Washington, D.C. or Chicago, or ...

GT 32:35 We have that revelation that says, Woe the City of New York and Boston[9] and...

---

[8] See https://www.churchhistorianspress.org/george-q-cannon?lang=eng

[9] D&C 84:114-115 says, "Nevertheless, let the bishop go unto the city of New York, also to the city of Albany, and also to the city of Boston, and warn the people of those cities with the sound of the gospel, with a loud voice, of the desolation and utter abolishment which await them if they do reject these things.

115 For if they do reject these things the hour of their judgment is nigh, and their house shall be left unto them desolate."

Christopher 32:39 Yeah, we become really uncomfortable with that one. In fact, in 1918, we have a discourse, this is one of the things that was a stir. Joseph F. Smith, denounces the White Horse prophecy, and in that same statement, he denounces this prophecy, one that's been credited to him, the 1877 prophecy of, this vision of walking through all these American cities and seeing them destroyed along the way. He says, "Don't trust this nonsense either." So these two things. I think that was really important, that Conference talk because it said the sort of destructions on America aren't the things you should be looking at. But, yes, a huge change, as we rethink this.

Christopher 33:24 These two other trajectories are--one, we see from a very, I call it "prophecy enthusiasts". So a segment of Latter-day Saints, who might hold on to some, although they're more likely to see themselves part of America, they might emphasize Cold War ideas or something like that. [These individuals] maintain some of the classic prophecies but just realize that they need to do so privately. This group, it's still possible to share visions privately and, in part of the book I argue that this is the case. Once, we were very vocal about personal visions, and personal dreams, and so on. Now, we've learned as part of the Americanization process, that Latter-day Saints need to just share them with loved ones. Don't announce them on the hilltops. That third trajectory is Mormon Fundamentalism, which actually holds on to that 19th century model of the United States, itself, being the bad guys, often.

GT 34:22 Yeah, that's a good overview.

Civil War Prophecy & Joseph's Apocalyptic Death

Introduction

One of the most famous prophecies of Joseph Smith is the Civil War prophecy, in which Joseph predicted the Civil War would start in South Carolina. When that happened a few decades later, how did that affect LDS apocalyptic thought? Dr. Christopher Blythe will let us know the answer. We will also talk about how Joseph Smith's death affected apocalyptic thought among the LDS. Check out our conversation....

Interview

GT 34:23 So I wanted to talk a little bit about some of these other periods, specifically, the martyrdom of Joseph Smith, because that was such a shock to the early saints. So, they now had to reinterpret that, in light of Joseph's death. Can you talk about how apocalypticism changed Latter-day Saint thought because of the martyrdom?

Christopher 34:51 Yeah, absolutely. One of the things I think is so interesting is that Latter-day Saints really emphasized a particular passage of The Book of Revelation. If you remember the Book of Revelation, there's this throne room vision. There's this book and this book has seven seals on it. Latter-day Saints say the seven seals represent time periods of the earth. But it seems like people have different opinions on that, but there are certainly major events occurring on Earth. As these seals are opened, you see the four horsemen are the first ones. Death, famine, and war being put out in these scenes. Then another seal is opened, and they see martyrs under the altar, this heavenly altar. And the martyrs are praying, and they're praying for vengeance. They say, "God, when will you avenge us?" The response is, "Be patient, wait until the rest of your brethren, the martyrs, have been killed." So Latter-day

Saints saw the scene and they said, "Well, one of the last days things is we're waiting for these martyrs to happen." Eliza R. Snow writes a poem that says, "Where are these martyrs?" We can expect persecution because it's happening. When the Saints first get to Nauvoo, Joseph's in Liberty Jail, and the Apostles write to the saints and say, "We know we're going to be persecuted, guys. This is part of the plan, and eventually, your murderers will be brought to justice." So, there's this expectation that the saints have to be martyred, that there should be widespread persecution, and it's part of bringing to pass the Second Coming. Joseph's death, one of the key things here is it changes all of that. Allegedly, one story is that Joseph, right before he goes to Liberty Jail, sends out a message for the saints to read that specific chapter about these martyrs, as he's on his way there. He wants them to be very aware of this idea of a last martyr. After his death--this is something that Sam Brown points out, Joseph is recognized in this role as last martyr. Now, all these events can happen.

Christopher 37:15 Brigham Young will give a discourse to say, "You don't understand what's happened here with Joseph's death. But because Joseph has died, there will be much less blood demanded of us." This sort of message to say, "We once expected vast martyrdom, but Joseph's actually been sort of a Savior to us physically, because the nation can be sated by taking his life. They're not going to come after us in the same way. That doesn't mean we don't want to leave town. But it's not demanded in the same way to fulfill these events." So, when I discovered that I thought, "This is incredible. What a sort of interesting idea of how martyrology plays here." Now, at the same time, that idea doesn't stick around too long. It's not one that's going to continue. Obviously, in 1857, those ideas pick up again, with the Utah War, and Parley P. Pratt's martyrdom and other things. Joseph's martyrdom becomes this major event, that now is going to bring up judgment on the United States, itself. So Brigham will emphasize, as sort of an idea that if these politicians hadn't directly conspired to kill Joseph Smith, if they didn't do that, they at least, were complicit in it, or they're happy that it happened. So, as a result, the judgment is going to pour out on Illinois and America. So, the flight from leaving Illinois into the desert or into the Rocky Mountains, is not just to get rid of your persecutors, it's to escape a nation that God is going to judge. So you need to get out of there.

GT 38:57 Well, yeah, there are a couple of directions that I want to go there. I know this wasn't in your book, but I think it's really interesting. When we look at the LDS Church's view that martyrdom is to be expected, trials are to be expected, but it's also interesting in that same time period, you have the Community of Christ. Well, I guess I should call it The RLDS Church, because they weren't the Community of Christ back then. The RLDS Church is saying, "Well, look. The reason why they're suffering so bad is because God's putting his punishments on them." William Bickerton is basically [saying] the same thing. It's funny, inside the church, we look at it as, "Oh, we're martyrs." Outside the church they're looking at it, "No, God's punishing you."

Christopher 39:45 Oh, isn't that fascinating? Yeah. The one thing I do mention with that is Strang's curse. Strang writes this curse on the Saints in Nauvoo predicting that they're going to get these same diseases and things that the Saints believe are being put on Joseph's persecutors and others, the idea of a curse. So, Strang, in 1845, is the first one to turn that on his fellow Latter-day Saints of how this is going to happen, "You guys are, are in trouble." So, absolutely.

GT 40:14 It's interesting to see how people interpret the same event.

Christopher 40:18 I think, one thing I didn't read about here is, for several these small groups, Brigham Young becomes the Antichrist figure. He's the one that's taken over the temple and done these evil things to lead astray the church. So, forget the United States government, they're not even part of it. They're looking at the tyrant of Brigham, rather than...

GT 40:38 Yeah, well, interesting. So, then, I think the next part that I--and you kind of alluded to it a little bit with the Utah War, but, of course, right after the Utah War was the Civil War. So, that brings up a whole lot of other [thoughts,] especially the Civil War, I really enjoyed what you talked about there, especially with the prophecy about the Civil War,[10] and how parts of it were fulfilled, and parts of it weren't fulfilled. Could you talk a little bit about that?

Christopher 41:03 Absolutely. I think the Civil War prophecy is perhaps one of the most important revelations Joseph Smith has. He is recording this 1832. Joseph, in 1832, gets nervous about spreading apocalyptic prophecies, particularly--the Book of Mormon is all about what Jared Hickman called Amerindian Apocalypse, the idea that this fallen people are going to be restored and part of the restoration is they're going to attack the Gentiles, and wipe out the nation. The nation is going to suffer from these Native American uprisings. Joseph says, "I want you guys to stop talking about it." We have this great letter where he says, "This is all true, but this is just going to make us enemies, if we talk too much about the curses on the nation," sort of thing. I think that plays into a really important decision. He wrote this amazing prophecy, and then they decided not to publish it. It doesn't show up in the Book of Commandments. It doesn't show up in 1835, or 1843, or 45 Doctrine & Covenants. It's going to wait all the way to be published until 1852 in the Pearl of Great Price.

Christopher 42:23 So, here's a revelation that Joseph and others had. It's maintained in our records, but not published to anyone, the Civil War prophecy. Joseph will still talk about it at various times. A few people have copies of it. Orson Pratt and Orson Hyde still have copies, but [it is] not published and distributed until 1852. Of course, that prophecy says there's going to be a north versus south fight that's going to start in South Carolina, the remnants, which should

---

[10] See D&C 87 found at https://www.churchofjesuschrist.org/study/scriptures/dc-testament/dc/87?lang=eng

the language of the time its Native American peoples are going to rise up, slaves will rise up against their masters. There's some major racial dimensions as well as regional dimensions to this Civil War. Eventually, Britain and other nations will get absorbed into this war. Eventually, it's going to fill the world until all nations are no more. So it can't all be fulfilled, right? We have this "nations are no more." There's a variety of other--the last couple of verses of this Section 87 are [read that] there are going to be floods and destructions, and all the other stuff you can imagine that are going to happen too. Nations will be no more. So, they can't all be fulfilled. That said, in 1852, the Latter-day Saints published this, and they get really excited as tensions fester between North and South. Later in the 1850s, Latter-day Saints are right there, pointing at these things. By the time 1860 rolls around, missionaries are writing Brigham Young, excited that they were able to get it published in different newspapers. So a lot of the Saints are flaunting this revelation everywhere they can go.

Christopher 44:13 There's been a non-historical criticism of this prophecy that says, "Oh, it was never a big deal until after the Civil War, because it wasn't added to the Doctrine & Covenants until 1876. But, once you understand this full picture, I mean, Latter-day Saints, hold it back and then in the 1850s, really just throw it in. This is used. We stopped doing missionary work in the nation for about a decade after Joseph Smith's death, and many people believe this is the end of missionary work to America, that they've had their chance. The nation's done. But around the time that Brigham Young announces polygamy, missionary work again opens up there. Orson Pratt is sent to Washington, D.C., and he starts a newspaper called *The Seer*. This is the second place the prophecy is published. His major use of that is to say, "Guys. We meant it. God is really going to judge the nation. So you need to get to the Rocky Mountains. We're gathering for a reason you need to get over here." So, I think it plays a major role, just among the Saints to get stragglers and new converts to get to Utah. It's fascinating. Of course, this is a major prophecy that Latter-day Saints are going to hold on to the whole way. Now, you mentioned that it didn't all happen the way they expected.

GT 45:42 Right.

Christopher 45:42 Certainly, Great Britain intercedes on the side of the South. So people can kind of point to that, but it doesn't seem like all the nations are part of this war.

GT 45:55 Yes.

Christopher 45:55 So how do you explain that? We're going to have thinkers like James Talmage and B.H. Roberts return to this prophecy in the early 1900s, with World War One and say, "Look, now these parts are fitting into place." Other people are playing with it in different ways. The big point from Brigham Young is, I think it's Brigham Young, maybe it's Heber C. Kimball. [One of them] says, "Look. It's not over yet. It seems like the division in the United States is at an end. But it's not. You can expect for that Civil War to pick up one more time."

GT 46:30 Maybe this year, right?

Christopher 46:31 Yes, maybe this year. Lots of people wanted to insert the idea of a second Civil War starting in Chicago. This is a late 1900s idea. [This idea] became particularly important nowadays as people pull to this one source from the 1900s. But just part of that bigger thing to say, the Civil War ended, but it's going to come back. Don't worry. One of the things I just thought was so interesting to research this is that this isn't just a Latter-day Saint conversation. The anti-Mormon press is also picking up on this and arguing, "Well, it does seem like you guys got this part right, but you didn't get this part right."

GT 47:14 Exactly.

Christopher 47:14 "And wait a second, this looks right, but come on." So, there's a great comment from Gunnison. Gunnison is a military guy who lives in Utah in the 1850s, and writes about his experience with Latter-day Saints. He writes his book that says, "Let's just hold off. If in a few years, angels lead the Latter-day Saints back across the plains to Jackson County, then we can trust all these other things."

GT 47:46 Well, yes, I thought that was interesting, because it did seem like there were ebbs and flows where there's a lot of apocalyptic thought. It was interesting to see how you talked about how lay members would sometimes publish the visions, and the church would encourage them, and other times they would discourage them. Even Brigham Young would discourage some of this apocalyptic thought. You mentioned something about, "A church needs moderation in these sorts of things." Can you talk a little bit more about that?

Christopher 48:16 Absolutely. The point about Joseph Smith, that he's even moderating some of these ideas--usually not, usually inviting people to have their own views. Certainly, based on his ideas, or speculation or sharing dreams, all things Joseph allows. Brigham Young also allows for those sorts of visions, broadly, if they're aimed at, "America or so on. They're going to have this bad thing happen here." Well, nobody's preventing those prophecies. But one prophecy that Brigham Young is very concerned about was a prophecy about how near the return to Jackson County would be. So, W.W. Phelps, and in particular, this idea of a prophet like unto Moses, who would lead them back there. Joseph's language in Section 58, I think it's 58, maybe it's 103. It talks about a prophet like unto to Moses, who will lead the people back to Jackson County.

GT 49:20 One mighty and strong.

Christopher 49:21 Yes, and later on the one mighty and strong, in Section 85, these sort of key figures that are going to come. The

Saints have to wonder, who are these guys? Are they the current prophet? Does that mean Rick Bennett could be the guy? All of a sudden, God tells you to do it and forget who's the leader of the church, now you're the guy.

GT 49:42 Some fundamentalists like to think that.

Christopher 49:44 Right, absolutely. People have the whole history of Latter-day Saints that have showed up for these messianic prophesied figures. Somebody is going to translate the Sealed Book of Mormon. Well, not Thomas S. Monson, it's me. It's not Russell Nelson, it's this guy. So these Messianic prophecies were dangerous because it did suggest to some people that maybe leadership could appear outside of just the basic succession. W. W. Phelps is a fascinating figure. He said that Brigham Young was the man who would lead the Saints back to Jackson County, the one like unto Moses. Brigham got very upset with W.W. Phelps. He calls him to a meeting and says, "Why would you think it's your place to publicly say, I'm the one with like Moses?" W.W. Phelps said, "I assumed it was Joseph before he died...

GT 50:35 It must be you.

Christopher 50:36 So it's you. Brigham Young says, "Well, why can't it be the guy after me, or the guy after him?" W.W. Phelps says, "I think it's nearer than that." Brigham Young says in this private meeting, "We're building the Salt Lake Temple. I don't think it's ever going to get built until we get back to Jackson County and build that temple first. I think we're going to be back there in seven years, but I would never tell the Saints that, because the second I tell them that, they're going to stop doing their work here, we're not going to build the temple. We're not going to build walls around our cities. We're just going to become focused on this idea." So, yes, I think that you're right, that key about moderation. How much apocalyptic should be encouraged is a major question for leaders then and, I think, now.

Apocalyptic World Wars

Introduction

Wars bring death, and with it, apocalyptic thought. In our next conversation with Dr. Christopher Blythe, we'll talk about how World Wars 1 and 2 affected LDS apocalypticism. We'll also talk about how Mormons thought the apocalypse was going to happen in 1890! Check out our conversation....

Interview

GT 51:25 Well, one of the interesting things that really kind of struck me in your book was this idea that around 1890--there was the prophecy that Joseph Smith would see God when he was 85 years old, which would have been about 1890. So, then there was this kind of resurgence of apocalyptic thought. Can you tell us more about that?

Christopher 51:49 Yes, absolutely. I think, leading up into the 1880s, there are several moments. In 1880, Wilford Woodruff himself is going to say in 1890, there'll be no more United States. People are really moving, but as they get closer to that date, people begin to become less certain. So, some scholars have pointed to the conference of October 1890, as the spot where leaders seem to be on either side of the issue. I don't think that's actually the case. I think when you get to that conference, really, the majority of leaders are just completely sold. The one sort of pro-1890 comments are more to say, "I think 1890 could be an important year, but we likely won't even understand the events that happen in 1890 until way after. Something might happen this year, but we won't recognize it," or something, "1890 is important, but really, every year is important until we get to the second coming. So don't just focus on this one." Wilford Woodruff comes with his revelation. He's seen Joseph Smith, and he's asked him, when's the second coming? Joseph Smith tells Wilford Woodruff, "I don't know. No man knows the day or the hour." So, you get the sort of shift. But, after 1890, I think people become, there's still some people that want to say, "What happened there?" The church doesn't want to come out and say this, but we get a lot of speculation. What did happen in 1890? Some people want to turn towards the ghost dance, which I think is fascinating.

GT 53:32 Also, we have the Manifesto in 1890, which is kind of a strange twist to this whole thing.

Christopher 53:38 Isn't that interesting? So that's the question. Is the issuing of the Manifesto[11] two months before Joseph's 85th birthday? Is that, maybe three months? Is that tied into our expectations of what's going on there? I don't know that it's tied to Wilford Woodruff who thinks, "We don't know the moment, but yeah, sure. It's coming really quick." But it might be certainly tied to the reception of the manifesto. The regular Latter-day Saints who had made plural marriage an essential part of their religion for the past 40 years, did they think "Oh, this isn't that big a deal? This is just government smokescreen, because we're right there. The Savior is going to come really quickly." So I think it's very possible.

GT 54:29 Yes. Well, then, of course, anytime we get into wars, you kind of mentioned World War I and World War II, those are some great times for apocalyptic thought. Can you talk about those time periods?

Christopher 54:41 Sure. World War I was a very important moment of Latter-day Saint apocalyptic and that's rethinking how we fit into the story. Ultimately, we were pacifists. The idea of Utah.... A great verse, I'm not going to remember where it is, says, "If you don't want to take up a sword in the last days flee to Zion." Zion is the place where there won't be war. Latter-day Saints don't fight wars. God defends their battles, and maybe they have to protect

---

[11] See https://www.churchofjesuschrist.org/study/scriptures/dc-testament/od/1?lang=eng

themselves defensively, but they're not going out to wage war. They are the place where people can be protected.

Christopher 55:30 It started with the Spanish-American War, Church leaders are saying, "Hey, you have your duty to fight for the nation, just like you had a duty to fight when soldiers came to Utah in 1857, for your faith." George Q. Cannon has taken that idea. In the Spanish-American War, we have Franklin Richards opposing that idea, saying, "No, we are pacifists, don't buy into that." But by the time we get to World War I, that's changed, for the most part, and leaders are encouraging Latter-day Saints to participate as good Americans. Now how does that make sense with prophecies about Zion, particularly, if this is the Last Days' war. I think it's fascinating.

Christopher 56:14 James Talmage and others begin to say, "We used to talk about Zion about us, but really Zion is the United States and this government of the United States. So they're Zion, and we can't be defeated because prophecies of Zion say, it can't be defeated. So if the United States is Zion, therefore, we're the winners here." It's really interesting. Now prophecy is occurring with us in place there. There is a great set of World War I prophecies from lay members of the church.

Christopher 56:50 LaRona Wilson is my favorite, I don't get to discuss her much in this book. I'm hoping I get to write a whole book on her, but she was a disabled prophetess who ran a dress making college in Cache Valley, who begins to prophesy about World War I. Her prophecies are about how if the Saints will immerse themselves in work for the dead, that they will be able to avoid actually having to go fight and they'll be able to win easily and so on in Europe, a whole slew. World War II is different. In some way--I got a great letter from someone, a well-known reporter, but I won't say her name, sent me this great letter quoting her grandparents, who talked about how the Prophet at the time was supposed to be the last prophet of the church, the prophet of World War II.

GT 58:00 That would have been Heber J. Grant, wouldn't it.

Christopher 58:02 Yes, and this is the seventh prophet, and so some people were making a big deal about how he's the last here. The letter says, "Now that we've passed this time period, what are we going to say to all these people who expected the Second Coming during his reign,? and that's related to World War II. I think World War II, of course, changes everything, though, for apocalypticism throughout America. Not only does it instigate the Cold War, but now we've seen the atomic bomb. The atomic bomb. You look at 19th century Latter-day Saint apocalypticism, and the emphasis is on disease, certainly on fighting amongst skirmishes and war, on racial conflicts. Now, 1945 shows up and all-American apocalypse turns towards this idea of fire. Now we understand how the globe could be burned. The atomic bomb becomes a major emphasis, not only in evangelical prophecy literature, but in our own.

GT 59:11 Yes. Well, interesting.

Bo, Rowe, & Pontius: LDS Apocalypticists

Introduction

We're moving into modern day apocalypticism. We're going to talk about 3 main figures: Bo Gritz, Julie Rowe, and John Pontius. Bo was former marine and Mormon convert who ran for president of the United States in 1992, receiving a significant number of votes in Utah. Julie Rowe currently has a YouTube channel where she shares her beliefs. John Pontius has written an influential book called Visions of Glory.[12] Dr. Christopher Blythe will tell us more about these recent figures. Check out our conversation....

Interview

GT 59:12 So as we move on from World War II, that kind of brings us up to the modern day. I remember reading your book and saying, "Oh, is he going to talk about Julie Rowe? Is he going to talk about John Pontius? Is he going to talk about Bo Gritz?" I was so happy that you talked about all three of them. So could you tell us a little bit more about how they relate to apocalypticism?

Christopher 59:35 Yes, absolutely. In the 1990s, Bo Gritz is a great representative, as well as guys like Jim Harmston, and others, of a Latter-day Saint who's become concerned about New World Order conspiracy theories. The United Nations, what role are they going to play in sort of setting up the scene for an anti-Christ figure and certainly our own distrust of the idea of the sort of global government? I just find that really interesting how Latter-day Saints turn in that direction as well. This is a moment where far right conservative, political ideas--John Birch Society is functioning in Utah and sometimes, John Birch Society isn't far enough for some

---

[12] Can be purchased at https://amzn.to/3k6ueyd

people in Utah County. So, we're having different groups forming here. One of my questions was, "Why wasn't Y2K more influential amongst Latter-day Saints?"[13]

Christopher 1:00:46 I think the book, Educated, that came out, I won't remember her name right now.[14] It was a bestseller, actually a great memoir. She talks about her father, who is a Latter-day Saint apocalypticist who emphasizes Y2K. His local community thinks he's wacko. It's just not having that same influence, where there's a lot of reasons and Latter-day Saints stuff, literature earlier, where you would think the year 2000 should be the year. I mean, why wouldn't Y2K fit into that idea? I think the answer is because in the 1990s, Bo Gritz, Jim Harmston, others of these major apocalypticists at the time, become regulated by Church leaders. Church leaders become very nervous, not in the year 2000, but in the early 90s, and they need to take on the far right.

GT 1:01:39 Just so people know, Jim Harmston broke away from the LDS Church and started his own fundamentalist group and became a prophet. I think, isn't that the True and Living Church of Jesus Christ of Latter-day Saints?

Christopher 1:01:54 Saints of the Last Days.

GT 1:01:56 Oh, so I got it wrong. Yeah. But then Bo Gritz actually ran for president and was quite popular in Utah. I know you said that some church leaders such as President Hinckley said, "We don't endorse this guy."

---

[13] Y2K stands for "Year 2000" and refers to a design problem in computers in which they only used 2 digits to represent a year. So when the dates on computers changed from 1999 to 2000, there was a chance computers would malfunction. Many businesses went to great expense to fix the flaw, and there were very few problems associated with it, but many experts warned of a computer apocalypse as the year 2000 approached.
[14] The author is Tara Westover and it can be purchased at https://amzn.to/3no6WWR .

Christopher 1:02:11 Right.

GT 1:02:12 Could you talk a little bit more about that?

Christopher 1:02:13 Right. So Bo Gritz discovers that he's been asked not to speak at Church events at the time he's running for president. He's an interesting figure. He's a former Green Beret running for president. In this sort of John Birch society, really anti-UN culture of the time, George Bush has given his speech around the Iraq War, where he talks about the New World Order. Many individuals worried about--the same sort of individual really worried during the Cold War about communism is now worried about the United Nations. So, he's running on those platforms: get the United States out of the United Nations.

GT 1:03:06 Which kind of repeats World War I with the League of Nations, because once again, there was a group of Mormons that hated it. So it's like history repeating itself.

Christopher 1:03:14 Yes, yes, yes, these are the same themes, 20th century apocalypticism and that sort of conservative impulse that goes along with some of these apocalyptic ideas is interesting because it has that ability to draw on a bigger crowd. You have different ways of reaching out to people and Bo Gritz learns how to do that. Bo Gritz was fascinating. Eventually he's going to want to teach survivalism, which is really important to these groups. Nowadays, we talk about preppers.

GT 1:03:48 It's the same sort of thing.

Christopher 1:03:49 Same sort of thing, although survivalists are going to be more into like, "Let's go out in the woods and practice shooting guns and stuff," whereas preppers may or may not be like that. He influences other groups. There's a guy in Utah County named Sterling Allen. Sterling Allen forms a group, really, from the sorts of people that were interested in Cleon Skousen, a little bit earlier, a little remnant there.

Christopher 1:04:19 He's filling up meetings throughout this area with hundreds of people who are promoting this idea of anti-UN things, the idea that the Second Coming is going to happen in 2000. There's going to be this corrupt government in place and so on, but really a way where you can take John Birch Society which is a non-denominational, largely Christian, but a non-denominational, far right group, and now it can become the American Study Group, which is explicitly LDS, and that movement. The Church wants to shut all of that down. So, in Sanpete County, where some of the stuff is prospering, as well as Utah County, there's a meeting of Stake Presidents, where they're directed on groups to be concerned with. Those are groups that are--one of the things they're doing is distributing Bo Gritz tapes. They're really focused on food storage. They're not keeping one year, they're going to next level. They homeschool their kids. They are members of the John Birch Society, and then did things that you would actually think they will be concerned about: and they have ties to polygamous groups, and they think Ezra Taft Benson is a silenced prophet, because he's not able to speak at church conference because of his health at the time, all sorts of things.

Christopher 1:05:46 So Church leaders have been tasked with finding and looking out for limiting the influence of these conspiratorially-minded prophecy enthusiast guys. I don't know if I'm so comfortable with looking out for negative influence amongst the populace. But I kind of understand the fear on all sides here in the 1990s. So, the Church is definitely clamping down on it. You jump on the other side of 2000, on the other side of 9/11, and we have a new rise of visionaries. Some fascinating things have happened. So the Bo Gritz camp has fallen to the side. From that, we have a really interesting movement that comes together, a prepper movement in the church, who probably share a lot of those sentiments. [They] will eventually, in the coming years, come together in a digital community called LDS AVOW, and a few other digital communities.

It lets us know the sort of size this movement, LDS AVOW is over 10,000 members.

GT 1:07:02 What does AVOW stand for?

Christopher 1:07:03 This is renamed from Parley P. Pratt's book, _Voice of Warning_.[15] So, now it's Another Voice of Warning. Of course, _Voice of Warning_ is this great, early apocalyptic book that Parley P. Pratt wrote that some people are even calling one of our standard works in the 1830s. You get the Book of Mormon, you have the Doctrine and Covenants, and you have _Voice of Warning_. Those are the most important things you can have. So this community comes together and from it, visionaries rise to the fore. It's interesting. You'd have these visionaries like Julie Rowe or visionaries like Sarah Menet, eventually, Chad Daybell. Spencer, who John Pontius writes his story, they all gain a lot of steam initially in these sorts of online communities. A guy like Spencer, actually they also write books and some of them get picked up. John Pontius' book, _Visions of Glory_ gets picked up at Desert Book and BYU Bookstore and sells hundreds of thousands of copies by becoming more mainstream that way.

Christopher 1:08:14 Others, like Julie Rowe, they don't get the same play at the larger bookstores and things, but this digital community makes it so a prophetic visionary could have a lot of influence, and through word of mouth, even, could just spread. I think these digital communities are also fascinating because you have these visionary figures, but you also have something that I think is much more sort of LDS, and that's sharing of visions and dreams. Starting around the turn of the century, Church leaders didn't say you're not allowed to have visions and dreams, or gifts of the spirit. You should have visions. You should have dreams, but you shouldn't share it. That's the great key, right? You share it with your family. You share it with trusted friends, as the Spirit tells you, and that's for multiple reasons, right?

---

[15] Can be purchased at https://amzn.to/2K6Y75s

Christopher 1:09:08 You want to treat this like it's sacred as the same way we treat the temples sacred by not speaking about it openly. But also, you want to make sure that no one will belittle it. So that idea, when you find a community of trusted friends, whether it's a study group, like the Manti study group that would be led by Jim Harmston would become this *True and Living Church*, or this digital community people feel comfortable in sharing their visions. So, there are these fascinating volumes. For a folklorist, this is just incredible-- volumes of people who, in this LDS AVOW community, who have shared their visions, and the community has recorded them so you can find books and, of course, they all come together like a glove. They are localized. We can expect a earthquake, and this is what the earthquake will do here, and I have this dream over here in Chicago. This is what's going to happen here, and so and so had a dream that the President will be assassinated and so they're weaving together all these dreams on the ground. These individuals, even the ones that really enjoy Spencer and Julie Rowe, they're going to consider themselves, with few exceptions, fully LDS. They even believe you should be cautious in sharing visions and things. They believe that if any of these people came out against the Prophet, they would respect the Prophet. So they don't see themselves as fringe or antagonistic. They just think everybody should be like them. We should all be piecing together our visions and realizing where we are in the last days timelines.

GT 1:10:54 Of course, Julie did get excommunicated just a few years ago.

Christopher 1:10:57 Yes, and this, this is what becomes interesting. In the book, I want to compare Spencer and Julie Rowe, because I think it's really important. [They are] two models of sort of prophets, lay prophets. One has become very, very successful Spencer..

GT 1:11:18 John Pontius.

Christopher 1:11:19 John Pontius wrote this book, *Visions of Glory*, which is Spencer's story of his near death experience. Then there's Julie Rowe, whose publisher Chad Daybell, helped her write several books about her experiences. Some people have wanted to say, the reason Spencer had so much more influence, particularly amongst mainstream Latter-day Saints, is because he was a man, Julie was a woman. I think that's related to what's going on here. But I actually think something else is going on here, because Spencer played the rules. The rules are, you don't want to become a celebrity, you're not trying to build a following away from the Church. He makes himself anonymous.

Christopher 1:12:06 His narrative is about how he actually had this vision and didn't share it until God told him to. He was friends with an apostle, and that apostle discouraged him from sharing it until he received revelation to do so. His details are so thoroughly--I mean, it's really a Last Days' event, that is about the power of the church, like the church coming together. I mean, he plays by all these rules, but the most important rule he does is he doesn't continue to write. He doesn't show up in podcasts. He doesn't have a website you can watch him. You can't send him money for energy work.

Christopher 1:12:53 Whereas Julie, and Julie would say, she's received direction to do this. Part of her message is what she's going to do. She's going to be this general in a Last Days' army, this nine-month war. She needs to prepare camps and gather supplies for individuals. She wrote multiple books. She started a YouTube channel. You can pay her a significant amount of money to have energy work done. I assume she's doing it for the best of reasons, but she's an entrepreneur. This is something that most Latter-day Saints would think is a little too close to being a paid preacher, or a little too close to being schismatic. So, I think it's interesting to piece those two together, and think why would one be prosperous in these stories and one not? Ultimately, it's interesting to me that these visionaries rise to popularity, and then they rise and fall. So, when one falls another shows up. I trace that most of these are based on near death experiences. So, I think it's interesting that Betty Eadie, the first major near death experience writer who wrote her own book, was a Latter-day Saint.

Christopher 1:14:25 She wrote Embraced by the Light,[16] and her story was just about the spirit world and things but [it was] first sold to Latter-day Saints, and then she got a major book deal so she took that first book and edited it to remove the Latter-day Saints elements, and then sold her near death experience to a wider market.

Christopher 1:14:46 She sets the space for several visionaries to show up later on, Latter-day Saint and not. In the Latter-day Saints circles we then had Gail Smith from here that gained a following by sharing her near death experiences on the radio. We then had Sarah Menet, who wrote a book very popular in the early 2000s.[17] She claimed to have seen 9/11 and other events. From Sarah Menet, we have a series of others until we got to Spencer, then Spencer--a lot of popularity. Julie Rowe. Julie Rowe declines in about 2015 and 2017, after she predicts an imminent earthquake, and certainly at her excommunication, where she's excommunicated for, really, energy work, it seems, as well as maybe some interactions with Church leadership stuff that might have played a role in it. But she's excommunicated, and then we have Chad Daybell.

GT 1:16:00 I'm glad... For people who don't know who Chad Daybell is, and that's quite a scandalous story. Julie did split from Chad essentially, right? She's kind of disavowed him.

Christopher 1:16:12 Yes. Oh, absolutely.

---

[16] Can be purchased at https://amzn.to/3pq0FeZ
[17] The book is called "There is No Death" and can be purchased at https://amzn.to/3pr92ac

Daybells & Zombie Apocalypse

Introduction

Chad Daybell has been in the news over the past year over the suspicious disappearance and deaths of his new wife Lori Vallow's children and relatives. We'll talk about their messages of apocalypticism with Dr. Christopher Blythe. Check out our conversation....

Interview

Christopher 1:16:13 The reason Chad Daybell does not play a role in this book is because he wasn't that controversial of a figure before this moment. He was a fiction novelist about Last Days. He was kind of like Timothy LaHaye, writing the Left Behind series for Christians,[18] the story of the rapture, and how do the left-behind new Christians deal with living in this apocalyptic world and trying to fight the Antichrist and so on. So he's writing various stories of Latter-day Saints who are living in the last days and the stories are very similar to the prophecies that have been given over time. He tells the story of a family in Springville and how it goes for them after this period. He's also publisher. He published Julie Rowe's accounts. He also published--I'm not going to remember her name right now. He published several visionaries over a decade or so, giving them a voice. His publisher really had a pretty good--they were the market for this Latter-day Saint Last Days material. Chad Daybell in 2017 comes out and says, "I was never just a novelist. I was actually a visionary and the things I was writing about, and these novels that I told you were fiction, are actually the story I've seen playing out. I'm this one father in the story, itself." The father, I mean, he was a leader who was going to kind of become like a Provo Temple President during the Last Days and things. So, he announced that he's this visionary. He claims that he had near-death experiences, a little unique near-death experience. He was cliff diving and had a

---

[18] Can be purchased at https://amzn.to/3no8LDb

rough fall. Although he didn't die, he was able to swim to shore, something happens. You have this huge fall, and he had this vision as part of it.

Christopher 1:18:40 That vision would relate to the Last Days and other things. So, Julie and Chad are friends, because he's her publisher. Julie is kind of dwindling. Chad publishes his autobiography and things we allege later, Julie's story is kind of developed here, because initially she's very supportive of Chad. We'll talk about why there would be a question of whether she'll be supportive in a second. She'll later her tell us that they kind of had a falling out for the last year, 2019, when they didn't have much contact. In 2019, Chad Daybell makes the news. Chad's wife has died suddenly in Springville. He marries a woman just a few weeks later, Lori Vallow.

Christopher 1:19:37 Lori Vallow's husband has been killed by her brother several months before and also two of her children are missing. It becomes a major case and rather than tell the whole story, I'll let your viewers and listeners look it up. But it becomes a major controversy. Chad and Lori are approached by the police. Where are these children? The grandma is very concerned. They say they're safe in Arizona with our friend. Please call the friend. It becomes known very quickly that the children are not there. Lori and Chad take off to Hawaii. Eventually they're tracked down there by reporters and the police have been watching them. Long story short, months go by. The prepper community who've been eating out of Chad Daybell's hands, excited to hear his visions and so on for a couple years now, defend him initially.   That includes Julie Rowe, who says that she's seen the children. They're fine. They're in Hawaii, too. Everything's great and certainly Chad didn't kill his wife.

Christopher 1:21:15 Really, there's a lot of support and so much so that there's a segment within this community that's absolutely appalled by the defense of Chad Daybell that says it doesn't make sense. Why would you not say where these two children are, an eight-year-old boy and a 16-year-old girl or 17-year-old girl? So, eventually, Lori Vallow is ordered to bring the children into court in Idaho. She refuses to do so. She gets arrested. Chad will later be arrested after the bodies of these two children are found on his property.

Christopher 1:22:01 The moment that happens--well, before, Julie will say she doesn't believe it anymore. She thinks that these children are dead and that Chad's done some bad things, at least. [She thinks Chad is] involved in these situations. She wanted to believe the other vision that she had had or experienced to discern it properly. She discusses this on a Lindsay Hansen Park interview.[19] So I don't want to put words into her mouth, but you can listen to it in more detail there. But she changes her mind on this. Chad, himself, has made a few statements when people accuse him of strange beliefs. He has said, and I think that really caused the rift between him and Julie in public sentiment, at least. He said, "I don't believe in any of these weird things. Those are all things Julie believes." The things were emphasis on past lives and emphasis on possession and emphasis on the idea that you might find out that although you're married to this person, two other women around here you've been married to in past lives or two other men.

GT 1:23:20 So kind of reincarnation kind of a thing.

Christopher 1:23:22 Certainly. Reincarnation is huge both for Julie and for Chad. There's really this sort of community of alternative writers among Latter-day Saints and Julie Rowe is certainly one of them. Douglas Mendenhall is another. There's a

---

[19] Lindsay has several interviews with Julie Rowe. Part 1 on Julie and Chad Daybell: https://www.yearofpolygamy.com/uncategorized/episode-180-julie-rowe-and-chad-daybell-part-one/
Part 2: https://www.yearofpolygamy.com/uncategorized/episode-180-julie-rowe-and-chad-daybell-part-two/ Another interview with Julie at https://www.yearofpolygamy.com/uncategorized/181-part-one-american-prophetess-an-interview-with-julie-rowe/ and https://www.yearofpolygamy.com/uncategorized/181-part-two-american-prophetess-an-interview-with-julie-rowe/

website that's anonymous. I'm not going to remember the title of the website, but I can find it for you later. It's a website that includes lots of visions and discussion of reincarnation in various estates. Also, the idea that the devil can be incarnated, too, in various states. [There is] a definite emphasis on conspiracy theory, modern Gadianton Robbers and a Last Days, imminent.

Christopher 1:24:13 But really an emphasis on demonology, the idea that we're all being--we see this most in Pentecostalism. I've been called out, because I've said a lot of Chad's beliefs people might think of Pentecostals before they thought of Latter-day Saints. In that, I meant this active emphasis on demonology. So, even Third Wave Charismatics, instead of Pentecostal sometimes. This idea of, we are all dealing with evil beings that might possess us but might also tempt us or assault us. In return, we need to use spiritual weapons, the helmet of Christ. [There are] all sorts of interesting symbols that are taken literally in this language. The devil has gotten me with a dart, and I'm hurt or sick, or he's put in a sort of explosive device. It's interesting material.

GT 1:25:26 Strange material.

Christopher 1:25:27 Strange material. It's the writings of Douglas Mendenhall. I don't think Chad is the only one. I think this is kind of a movement of writers, emphasizing these ideas: reincarnation, demonology, conspiracy theory. The idea of portals was a big point, the idea of translation, becoming immortal. All of these ideas are being promoted by these different authors. There are probably a group of 1000 people that read it. But, in the case of Chad Daybell, it seemed to come up with some terrible results. So, at this point, children have been discovered. Julie has disavowed him, as has the prepper community. We'll see what happens in court. But it would appear that from interviews around that, Lori, Chad's new wife had come to believe that her children were zombies. Their term for zombie meant that you'd become possessed so much, that your own spirit couldn't possess your body again. Your spirit's stuck out there in sort of limbo and now your body is being used by something evil. So you're no longer Rick Bennett, you are, fill in the blank.

GT 1:26:53 One of her children had autism. Is that correct?

Christopher 1:26:56 I think that's right. Yeah, this child, and she saw that his behavior, allegedly, on his last day on earth, his behavior, she claimed, telling her friend Melanie, that he had climbed up onto a ledge and knocked over a picture of Jesus. He was acting bizarre, and she believed this was a sign that he was possessed. We'll see what's determined, but usually they would pray. So, every day they would pray to get rid of all the zombies in the world. According to Melanie Gibb, who was a friend at the time, they could then say, "This morning, there was 1000 zombies in the world. But now there's 940. So we know that our prayers, wiped out 60 zombies," that sort of thing. But, in this case, it seems like they were more proactive in ridding the world of zombies.

GT 1:27:55 This is a terrible story.

Christopher 1:27:56 It is a horrible story. As I write about this, I had a professor I worked with that was listening to an interview I did on Chad Daybell the other day said, "Chris it's just too disgusting. This sounds like a second book, but you don't want to write that book. It's just sickening."

GT 1:28:19 Yes, It's terrible.

White Horse Prophecy

Introduction

Many people have heard about the White Horse Prophecy, but few people understand the details. Did you know it has been disavowed by LDS Leaders? In our next conversation with Dr. Christopher Blythe, we'll dive in deep to this well-known but misunderstood prophecy and discuss the ties to Mitt Romney. Check out our conversation....

Interview

GT 1:28:20 Well, let's move on. I probably could talk forever on this book. But the one issue that I really wanted to cover was the White Horse Prophecy, especially how it relates to Mitt Romney. Because I think a lot of people have heard about the White Horse Prophecy. Of course, I have, but I didn't understand it in quite the detail. I thought you gave some really good detail about it. Can you first tell us what is the White Horse Prophecy, what it's about? And then talk about how it tied into Mitt Romney's campaign?

Christopher 1:28:59 Absolutely. The White Horse Prophecy today, when someone talks to someone else about the White Horse Prophecy, they usually think it's just this one brief prophecy, which is that the constitution will hang by the thread. There will come a moment that the Constitution is imperiled, and usually today, people think this will be that a Latter-day Saint, maybe a Latter-day Saint politician is going to fix that. The church has come out against the White Horse Prophecy, so people thought the Church has come out against this idea, that the constitution will hang by a thread.

Christopher 1:29:37 In actuality, we jump back to 1840, Joseph Smith publicly taught this idea that the constitution would be imperiled, and that the Latter-day Saints, not one individual, but the Latter-day Saints would play a role in protecting it. Brigham Young talks about this in 1855 and Eliza R. Snow talks about it. This is just a really common prophecy. I mean, this is the theme of the book: America has failed. They've killed the Prophet Joseph Smith. Latter-day Saints have moved--and they've taken away the basic freedom of religion and freedom of expression and speech and so on. We can maintain all these things in Utah. By going to Deseret, the Rocky Mountains, we can build a society that protects the Constitution.

Christopher 1:30:24 So for most Latter-day Saints at that time, they would think this concept, this prophecy has already been fulfilled. We're here protecting the constitution that they rejected. So this prophecy's out there. In 1902, Edwin Rushton is a fascinating individual. Edwin Rushton is one of these guys that had a seer stone his whole life and would find lost objects for people. He thought that one side of his seer stone could tell you about the spirit world and one side could tell you about the Lost 10 Tribes. [He was a] fascinating individual. Edwin Rushton, in 1902, sits down and records a very lengthy sermon of vision that he saw along with another guy, Theodore Turley, in Nauvoo. We don't have a statement from Turley about it. But he called it the White Horse Prophecy. He said in 1843 Joseph Smith gave this prophecy and it was a sermon, that he'd seen a vision of the Four Horsemen of the Apocalypse.

Christopher 1:31:25 The first four seals are opened in this book in heaven, and each one, as they're opened, a rider appears on a different colored horse. There's a pale horse. There's a white horse. There's a red horse, and there's a yellow horse. Excuse me, there's a black horse, not a yellow horse. Each of them--and the book represents-- in Revelation, represents different sort of judgments, famine, death, war, that are going to come out upon the land in the last days or, if you're a literalist in Joseph Smith's interpretations, you think maybe they came out on the earth at different time periods already. But, according to this source in Edwin Rushton, Joseph said, "In the Last Days, I'm going to tell you what's going to happen. I'm going to tell you about these four horses. The white horse is the Saints. The Pale Horse are those guys that look like us, but aren't actually us, the Gentiles, the Americans. The Red Horse are Native Americans, and the black horse are African Americans, former slaves, or slaves at the time. I'm going to tell you the story about these four guys.

Christopher 1:32:46 So, the story of the White Horse prophecy is recorded in 1902. It's largely based on the Civil War Prophecy. It has an idea that the Gentiles are going to attack the Saints. actually, all sorts of wars are occurring here. It begins with this reference that says there'll be a terrible revolution in the land that leaves the United States without any supreme government. So, great, wild moment's going to happen. Ultimately, the Constitution is going to hang by a thread. In the White Horse Prophecy, it's not a politician that saves it either. The Red Horse, the Native Americans align with the White Horse, the Mormons are going to join together, and they're going to preserve the Constitution. Anyways, the White Horse prophecy was very prevalent for about 20 years and even into the 50s. I mean, the White Horse Prophecy is very popular.

GT 1:33:46 So just quickly; he wrote it down in 1902, but, supposedly, this had happened decades earlier.

Christopher 1:33:51 Yes, and this would make sense. I mean, in 1840, Joseph Smith did make a prophecy with the Constitution. Every other element of the White Horse Prophecy document he wrote, you could find somewhere else. Some of the specifics like an invasion from China on the West Coast, the same time there's an invasion from European forces on the east coast.

Christopher 1:34:19 You could find similar things in Joseph's teachings. I don't know one specifically about a Chinese invasion, but that was showing up at the time. But I call it a composite document. So, kind of like if you thought of one of the Gospels, being a variety of stories told about the Savior. They're then being pulled together for this one text or even these four Gospels and you're pulling them together to make the Gospels of the New Testament. The White Horse prophecy is someone pulling together the sayings of Joseph Smith and framing them as if they happened all at this one moment in 1843. Apparently, believing that this guy 60 years later could remember word for word Joseph's prophecy. This is published and spread as Joseph Smith's most important prophecy, Joseph Smith's greatest teaching. You get your pamphlet, or you'd write out your version of the White Horse Prophecy.

Christopher 1:35:19 Now, today, everybody has forgotten the actual document of the White Horse Prophecy. Very few people know or have read the White Horse Prophecy, itself. Instead, they just know this phrase: "The Constitution will hang by a thread, and one of the elders will save it." At some point, this took on a political dimension. In 1896, when statehood happens in Utah, there's an idea that Latter-day Saints could participate within the nation to protect the Constitution. That's key. So, we've switched from that idea that we're going to save it over here all by ourselves. Now, we're going to save it as part of the nation. Ezra Taft Benson, this prophecy is emphasized throughout [his life]. There's even, in 1940, the Church has denounced the White Horse Prophecy. And, because people already are thinking the Constitution prophecy is the most important thing about that thing we're waiting for, in 1940, Charles Nibley writes an article in *The Improvement Era* that says, "I keep hearing people say we no longer believe the Constitution will hang by a thread."

Christopher 1:36:30 He says, "That's not the case at all. Look at all these statements. I don't know who's saying this to people, but this just isn't true." So, the Church is coming back and saying, "No, we really do believe in the Constitution Prophecy." Now, you jump forward in our day, and we have statements from the Church, discounting it, the Constitution Prophecy, because of this confusion. Is it the Constitution, or is it the White Horse Prophecy? Ezra Taft Benson is quoting it over conference, and it's really with the rise of Mitt Romney, where we've become really concerned on how the rest of the world is interpreting the White Horse Prophecy. Today, of course, the White Horse Prophecy, when someone says it, just means there's going to be this Mormon politician that shows up to save the day when the Constitution is imperiled. Now we use it for Mitt Romney, initially, the idea that Latter-day Saints were more prone to elect a Latter-day Saint politician because they believe in this prophecy. Mitt Romney would come out and say, "That whole idea is folklore."

GT 1:37:39 Right up your alley.

Christopher 1:37:39 Right up my alley. Others, Sally Denton wrote this terrible article in Salon,[20] in which she says, "Pay attention to this White Horse Prophecy, because all Mormons believe it. You don't want a president who has this sort of religious apocalyptic vision of why he should lead the nation." She's not saying that, but the idea would be we had that with Ronald Reagan, and so on. We don't want to have that situation.

Christopher 1:38:14 It's fascinating. I end this book by talking about her prejudicial article, and then, a great defense written, critical of her approach, taken both by a Latter-day Saint law scholar Nate Oman, but also a great Jewish scholar writing in a Jewish newspaper saying, "This is just, if you take *Protocols of Zion*, this sort of anti-Jewish manual reads really similar to Sally Denton's radical claim that a Latter-day Saint politician is trying to lead the world by getting elected to the United States Presidency. So, it's fascinating.

Christopher 1:38:58 The White Horse Prophecy still shows up in conversation around Mitt Romney. I'm going to be honest. I've not met a Latter-day Saint who--I've seen many Latter-day Saints ask the question, "Could Mitt Romney actually do this?" I've never seen a Latter-day Saint say, "Chris, I think Mitt Romney is going to fulfill this prophecy."

---

[20] See
https://www.salon.com/2012/01/29/mitt_and_the_white_horse_prophecy/

Christopher 1:39:17 I just haven't. I know some people have told me they have. In any case, it's usually used at this point, to kind of make a joke, like, finally Mitt is going to stand up to Trump and save the Constitution. I think it's very interesting. White Horse Prophecy was denounced in 1918. This Constitution part is not [denounced.]

GT 1:39:44 The Constitution still could hang by a thread.

Christopher 1:39:46 Yes, the Constitution, well, it's been repeated by Latter-day Saint prophets for over 100 years, up to the late 1980s, and never been disavowed. Certainly, it could still hang by the thread. It was never going to be fixed by a Latter-day Saint politician. That was never the claim. Ezra Taft Benson said it was going to be fixed by Latter-day Saints participating in politics, like all of us need to go out and vote sort of thing and to stand up for the Constitution and democracy.

GT 1:40:16 Of course, he ran for president, as well. So, could he be the White Horse? (Chuckling)

Christopher 1:40:21 There's a lot of people that could be the White Horse, but not really. I think the actual story the White Horse Prophecy documents is just so fascinating. I mean, this is the idea that Latter-day Saints are building a utopia, in which, when the rest of the world falls apart, people can flee here and be protected. Then when forces come to mess with Zion that's established, Native Americans working together, will defend themselves. The United States, those that are righteous can also take refuge here in this spot. So, I like the message. Unfortunately, part of the message is that racial dimensions in the United States are going to lead to its downfall. There's going to be a race war. Blacks and Native Americans versus Gentiles are a major part of the story and Latter-day Saints are portrayed as the good guys that can help everybody preserve a nation that's had its come-uppance.

GT 1:41:35 Interesting. What would you say to people who believe in this now? Is there going to be an apocalypse? Are we on the edge of destruction? I have family members that are like, "We should [be prepared."] I'm not saying this is bad advice, [we should] make sure that we have our year's supply, and this sort of a thing. But do some people go too far with that?

Christopher 1:42:03 I think yeah. I think people can go too far. I think we want to be balanced. I think, the advice of Latter-day Saint leaders that say, "Stay in the safety of the center of the gospel, don't go out on the fringes," is wise. I don't think there's anything unhealthy. I think it's a good thing to store up. If somebody has six months, a year, two years, I don't care, supply of food in their homes. I think it's a great thing. I always think it's weird, the conversation where people say, "and I don't want to share this food come these bad moments in the future." I think we can get weird in those sorts of things. But if you want to prepare, I think that's a great idea. If you want to build a garden that you tend, so you're not just using stores, that sounds really cool. I wish I had my garden setup like that. So I think preparation, learning survival skills, being a good boy scout, those things like these are kind of cool.

Christopher 1:43:11 At the same time, I think people can, can begin to live their lives in fear. I think a lot of government things are corrupt. But I think if I saw my daily interactions with everyone as part of a conspiracy, it might have a negative effect in my life. I also think, at the end of the day, Latter-day Saints have often prepared for the Second Coming, but very rarely have Latter-day Saints ever, well, at least as far as church goes, ever promoted the idea that the Second Coming was imminent, as in a few years. It's always been a couple generations away. We're preparing for the Second Coming, and we're doing our best and we're living with that optimism, not that negativity. We don't emphasize the idea that destructions are going to happen on our neighbors or something like that. We're hoping that we can see this great Zion established, the idea of the Savior returning. I think that's an absolutely wonderful mindset to have, that we're living to prepare the world, for the great coming of Christ and through his leadership and directions, all the bad things like disease and racism and prejudices and social classes, poverty and so on, will all go away.

Christopher 1:44:45 This sort of perfect world will come into being. I think that's a really cool mindset. I live like that. I'm a Latter-day Saint and a convert and I like the idea that my tradition teaches that we're in the last days. We have a destiny. There's something we're doing. Now, I also live. I don't expect to be alive when the Second Coming happens, but I could, and I would like it that way. But I also want to prepare to meet God whenever I die. So, I live my life also with knowledge that my Second Coming could be anytime, based on based on my mortality. So, in short, I think these things could become negative, if people allow them to become conspiratorial and paranoid and shut themselves off from society, all those things. Or, one of the worst stereotypes of this is that it could lead to violence. Well, unfortunately, we know some historical events where it has led to violence. So, certainly, I would want to hold onto that early Latter-day Saint vision of pacifism. Right, we are the ones that get to escape that violence. Anyways, it's a potentially negative force, that can also be a great optimism. That's the side that I think Latter-day Saints promote now, and hopefully will continue to promote for the foreseeable future.

GT 1:46:19 Cool, cool. Was there anything we missed that you want to tell us about or any new projects you're working on?

Christopher 1:46:27 I am working on a project that I'm very excited about right now. It's a reception history of Emma Hale Smith. I'm a few chapters into it, and I'm loving it. So, probably by the time this this shows up on the internet, and in the podcast, a segment of it'll be published on the Center for Latter-day Saint Arts, which looks at how Emma Smith has been portrayed in theater. This is kind of fun.

GT 1:46:57 Oh, wow. Interesting. All right. Well, Dr. Christopher Blythe, I really appreciate you being here on *Gospel Tangents*. Thanks a lot.

Christopher 1:47:06 Thanks so much, Rick. It's great.

Additional Resources:

Check out our other interviews with Dr. Matt Harris on President Benson and his apocalyptic beliefs.

Part 2 of our conversation with Dr. Matt Harris from CSU-Pueblo. This time we discuss the political and spiritual life of Ezra Taft Benson.

255: Hoover on MLK & ETB
https://gospeltangents.com/2019/03/hoover-on-mlk-etb

254: How Hinckley Prevailed over Benson on Civil Rights
https://gospeltangents.com/2019/03/hinckley-prevailed-benson-civil-rights/

253: The End of Benson's Political Aspirations
https://gospeltangents.com/2019/03/end-bensons-political-aspirations/

252: Benson on Civil Rights & Communism
https://gospeltangents.com/2019/02/benson-civil-rights-communism/

251: Benson and John Birch Society
https://gospeltangents.com/2019/02/benson-john-birch-society/

250: How Ezra Taft Benson Joined Eisenhower
https://gospeltangents.com/2019/02/how-ezra-taft-benson-joined-eisenhower-part-8-of-13/

Last Thoughts

You can get our transcripts at our amazon.com author page. I've got a link here, but just do a search for Gospel Tangents interview, and you should be able to find a bunch of them there. Please subscribe at Patreon.com/gospeltangents. For $5 a month, you can hear the entire interview uncut and for $10 you can get a pdf copy. We've also got a $15 tier where if you want a physical copy, I'll be the first to send it to you, so please subscribe at Patreon or on our website at Gospeltangents.com. For our latest updates, please like our page at facebook.com/Gospeltangents and also check our twitter updates Gospel tangents. Please subscribe on our apple podcast page tinyurl.com/GospelTangents, or you can subscribe on your android device. Just do a search for Gospel Tangents. Thanks again for listening. Click here to subscribe, here for transcript and over here we've got some more of our great videos. Thanks again.

www.ingramcontent.com/pod-product-compliance
Lightning Source LLC
Chambersburg PA
CBHW061525250726